DON'T EAT THIS BOOK

HA HA HA BURP CRUNCH YUM

CREATE IT, MAKE IT YOURS...

DAVID SINDEN & NikalaS CatLOW

PSS!
Price Stern Sloan
An Imprint of Penguin Group (USA) Inc.

PRICE STERN SLOAN
Published by the Penguin Group

Penguin Group (USA) Inc., 375 Hudson Street, New York, New York 10014, USA

USA | Canada | UK | Ireland | Australia | New Zealand | India | South Africa | China
Penguin Books Ltd, Registered Offices: 80 Strand, London WC2R 0RL, England

For more information about the Penguin Group visit penguin.com

Published in Great Britain in 2012 by Red Fox, an imprint of Random House Children's Publishers UK. A Random House Group Company.

Text and illustrations copyright © 2012 by David Sinden and Nikalas Catlow. All rights reserved. First published in the United States in 2013 by Price Stern Sloan, a division of Penguin Young Readers Group, 345 Hudson Street, New York, New York 10014. PSS! is a registered trademark of Penguin Group (USA) Inc. Printed in the U.S.A.

10 9 8 7 6 5 4 3 2 1

ISBN 978-0-8431-7326-0

PEARSON

ALWAYS LEARNING

LEGAL DISCLAIMER

HAVE FUN WITH THIS BOOK, BUT ALWAYS EXERCISE GOOD COMMON SENSE AND AVOID DOING ANYTHING DANGEROUS. SO DON'T BREAK A LEG BEING SILLY WITH IT THEN GO CRYING TO YOUR MOM. READING IT UNDER WATER IS A BAD IDEA, TOO, AS IS COLLIDING WITH IT AT A HUNDRED MILES AN HOUR OR GLUING YOUR FACE TO IT. TRY NOT TO TRIP OVER IT, AND NEVER LET IT BURN AND SET FIRE TO YOUR HAIR. IT'S PROBABLY BEST TO WEAR A HELMET AND ELBOW PADS WHILE READING IT — JUST TO BE ON THE SAFE SIDE. (SERIOUSLY THOUGH, EXERCISE REASONABLE CARE FOR YOURSELF AND OTHERS WHILE USING THIS BOOK.)

WHAT IS THIS BOOK?

This book is totally awesome and a bit ridiculous. There's LOADS of stuff to do in it - WILD, creative stuff. It's fun, and you'll LOVE it!

RULES FOR USING THIS BOOK:

RULE ONE - DON'T EAT THIS BOOK.

RULE TWO - THERE ARE NO MORE RULES.

RULE THREE - RULES SUCK.

SO WHAT DO I DO?

Do absolutely anything you like, except eat it!
Each page is for you to mess with,
for your thoughts,
for your amusement.

This book is all about YOU.

IDENTIFY YOURSELF

Fill this page with your name, as many times and in as many styles as you like.

Olivia

A SELF-PORTRAIT

Draw OR paint a self-portrait wearing a blindfold.

GET PHYSICAL

Be daring with this book. If you want to tear something out, tear it out; don't worry about what's on the other side of the page – it's OKAY, it's **THAT** sort of book! If you want to stick something in, stick it in. Draw what you want. Scribble what you want. Write what you want. Fill it with ideas, color, and noise. Take it everywhere, show everyone, and share it if you want.

TO LOOSEN UP, TRY THESE THINGS:
See how good they feel!

CLOSE THE BOOK. DRUM ON IT. WRITE YOUR NAME ON THE COVER AND CHANT REPEATEDLY: "THIS BOOK IS MINE, ALL MINE – I CAN DO WHAT I WANT!"

ADD COLOR

WIPE JELLY, TOOTHPASTE, OR ANYTHING HERE:

Scribble outside the dotted lines.

Rip this bit off and throw it away. (Don't worry about what's on the back.)

Tape or glue an object here:

CAN YOU BALANCE THIS BOOK ON **THE TIP OF ONE FINGER?** CAN YOU SPIN IT?

FOOT ART

Now that you've loosened up, take off your shoes and socks, and use your feet to draw and paint here with wild abandon.

CAN YOU DO THESE?

Can you carry this book on your head?
Can you keep it there while standing on one leg?
. . . while running on in place?

Can you balance it on one finger?
. . . on your chin?
. . . on your elbow while doing the chicken dance?
. . . on your shoulder while shrugging?
. . . on your foot while turning in a circle?
. . . on the back of your hand while clapping loudly?
. . . on your bottom while walking on all fours?

Can you catch it on your knee?
. . . and keep it there while hopping?

If you do touch it, then
you _ _ _ _ _ _ _ _ _ _ _ _ _ _ _ _ _

_ _ _ _ _ _ _ _ _ _ _ _ _ _ _ _ _ _

_ _ _ _ _ _ _ _ _ _ _ _ _ _ _

How many different marks can you make on these pages? Use different tools, such as pens, pencils, brushes, and uncommon painting tools like sticks, string, cardboard, leaves and stones. Make lines, dots, scratches, stains, erasings, rubbings, and anything else you wish.

squish things HERE...

Can you decorate this page with stains and splats?
Create by squishing peas, gum, and berries — any
other ideas?

Draw a picture of someone you would
like to slap, but wouldn't.
SLAP IT.

Take this book outside and create a picture on these pages by applying color or mud with bouncing balls: rubber balls, tennis balls, footballs — you choose!

REMOVE THIS PAGE BIT BY BIT USING ONLY A HOLE PUNCH.

Use the bits to decorate the front cover.

FOLD THIS PAGE IN HALF AS MANY

TIMES AS YOU CAN.

Can you do seven folds?

MAKE THIS STRIPY

This page is for stripes: colored stripes, black stripes, textured stripes, fat stripes, all the same stripes, or every stripe different – you choose!

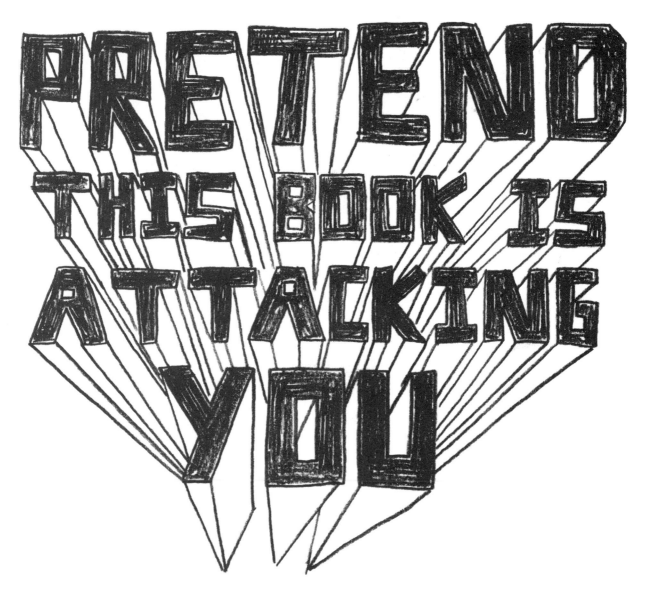

. . . AND SEE IF ANYONE NOTICES!

HELP!

the LA-LA SONG

Finish writing the "La-la" song — the song that gets on everyone's nerves. Sing it until people can take no more.

La-la-la-la-la . . .

DRAW HOW YOU'LL LOOK AT 100 YEARS OLD.

Create an energetic image using rubber bands.
Dip them in paint and fire them at these pages.
Stretch them! Shoot them! Or glue them on!

Bling these pages using tinfoil,
metallic pens, paper clips,
staples, glitter, etc.

YOU CREATE IN THIS DIRECTION.
Use an unusual drawing tool, such as a
borrowed lipstick or eyebrow pencil.

YOUR FRIEND CREATES IN THIS DIRECTION.
Add as many colors to the picture as you can.

CAN  YOU READ THIS?

W

HE

NYO

UCONC

ENTRATET

OREADTHISYO

USTARTTOSQUIN

TANDWHENYOUSTARTSQUI

NTINGITLOOKSLIKEYOUARECONSTIPATED

 ← Here's a prune for you!

KEEP THIS PAGE IN THE BATHROOM TO SCRIBBLE ON OR IN CASE YOU RUN OUT OF TOILET PAPER . . .

HURRY UP IN THERE!

I'M DOING SOMETHING.

CORRECT ✓ THIS

Can you correct these famous words of wisdom?

A BIRD IN THE HAND IS WORTH TWO IN THE TOILET
DON'T COUNT YOUR TOILETS BEFORE THEY HATCH
THE BIGGER THEY ARE, THE HARDER THEY TOILET
DON'T BITE OFF MORE THAN YOU CAN TOILET
A FOOL AND HIS TOILET ARE SOON PARTED
NEVER BITE THE TOILET THAT FEEDS YOU
YOU CAN'T JUDGE A TOILET BY ITS COVER
DON'T LOOK A GIFT HORSE IN THE TOILET
DON'T PUT ALL YOUR EGGS IN ONE TOILET
BETWEEN A TOILET AND A HARD PLACE
A LEOPARD CAN'T CHANGE ITS TOILET
TOILETS SPEAK LOUDER THAN WORDS
WEAR YOUR HEART ON YOUR TOILET
LET THE CAT OUT OF THE TOILET
DON'T CRY OVER SPILLED TOILETS
CURIOSITY KILLED THE TOILET
BARKING UP THE WRONG TOILET
A TASTE OF YOUR OWN TOILET
RAINING CATS AND TOILETS
COUNT YOUR LUCKY TOILETS
YOU ARE WHAT YOU TOILET
WATER UNDER THE TOILET

AS SICK AS A TOILET
SAVED BY THE TOILET
OVER MY DEAD TOILET
A CHIP ON YOUR TOILET
NEW KID ON THE TOILET
IT TAKES TWO TO TOILET
THE ICING ON THE TOILET
LET SLEEPING TOILETS LIE
THE BALL IS IN YOUR TOILET
HIT THE TOILET ON THE HEAD

MAKE THIS

BEASTLY

"It had the head of one creature, the body
of another, and the legs of a third!"
Add special features such as tentacles, horns,
wings, whatever. Name your beast.

WRITE A SECRET OVER AND OVER UNTIL
NO ONE CAN READ IT.

PSYCHEDELIC POOP

Imagine a parrot that poops in bright colors. How would this page look if it had been left below the parrot's perch?

THROW THINGS AT YOUR WALL

AT YOUR WALL

GRAFFITI IT

SHOUT, USING ANY PAGE AS A MEGAPHONE.
THINGS TO SHOUT MIGHT INCLUDE:

"Head lice, head lice. Come and get your head lice!"
(While scratching.)

"Get out of my personal space!"

"Everybody break-dance!"

"Look there's . . . [someone famous]!"

"I HAVE RABIES!" (With toothpaste around your mouth.)

"Will you be my fwiend?"

"Iced ink."

"Move away from the vehicle!"

"Hoof hearted."

"It wasn't me."

SHOUT THIS

"Stay off my property!"

"Hands up if you're wearing clean underwear!"

OR YODEL, OR GARGLE, OR BURP.

Draw here by holding a pen or paintbrush still and moving the book instead.

CREATE A . . .

RANSOM note

WHAT WOULD THIS PAGE LOOK LIKE IF IT HAD BEEN USED AS A

FLY SWATTER?

ESCAPE FROM THIS PAGE

Try to scratch through this page
using only your fingers.

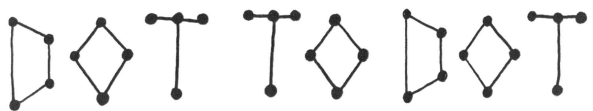

Connect the dots in any order. Change color and connect them again in a new order. Do this over and over to create a design. Fill in any shapes you wish.

LIST THIS

PETS YOU'VE HAD OR WANT:

YOUR BEST QUALITIES AND SKILLS:

YOUR TOP TEN SONGS:

THINGS YOU GOT INTO TROUBLE FOR:

BOOKS YOU'VE READ:

COUNTRIES YOU'VE VISITED:

PLACES YOU'VE BEEN SICK:

PEOPLE YOU'VE KISSED:

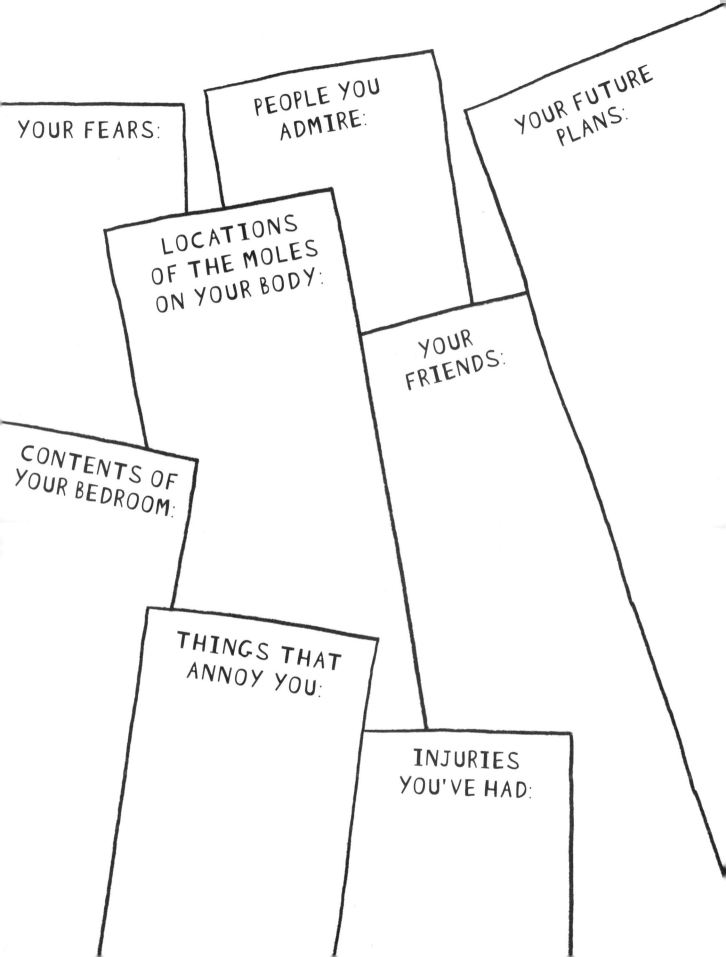

DRAW HOW YOU WOULD LOOK
IF YOU WERE A DOG.

A MUSTACHE A DAY,
FOR A WEEK.

Refine them. Design your own. Try them on.

DRAW AROUND ROUND THINGS.

Find round objects. Draw around them lots of times to create a pattern. Color where they overlap.

THIS ISN'T A LETTER L.

It's part of something else. **YOU** decide what it is.

THIS IS THE BOGEYMAN.

What does he look like?

Use this page to let out your anger. Vent it here:
Write your thoughts, say the things you want to
say but shouldn't. Draw your anger, then scribble
it out, erase it. See how much better you feel!

BITE THIS

Add mosquito bites or vampire bites.
Draw how they look, make holes — attack!

PLEASE BE GENTLE!

DRAW A HEADACHE

On these pages, create a big picture of
what a headache feels like.

USE THIS BOOK TO  SOMEONE

If someone touches it, "tut" loudly, then spray it with disinfectant.

Keep opening it and peering inside saying, "Are you okay in there?"

Give it to someone and ask them to find the idiot page.

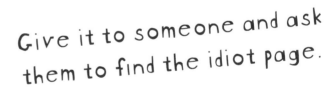

Act as if you're reading it and, each time you turn a page, do the following: Laugh hysterically, snort, scream, "AAARGH! MY EYES!" then pretend to get an electric shock.

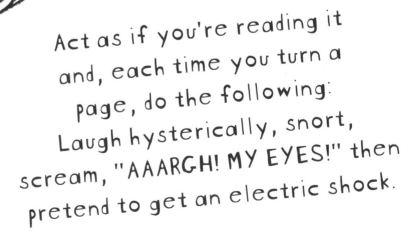

Show it to someone, frown, then whisper
in a ghostly voice, "Death by paper cuts."

Pretend it weighs too much and keep dropping it.
Then fall down as you try to pick it up.

Make explosion noises when anyone goes near it.

Every time someone speaks, slam the book
shut and say, "Well, that's that then!"

Leave it in the way. When someone goes to
pick it up, say, "Hey, that's mine!"

Stand next to someone and fan the air with it.
Say to them, "Did you have to do that?"

Sit at your desk with it, chuckling. When someone
comes to see, ask them if they have an appointment.

Read it using binoculars. When someone questions you,
reply, "Aye, aye, Captain," to anything they say.

Leaf through it, sniffing each page
and mumbling, "Mmm, bananas."

THIS IS A COMIC

Add your own words.

Add your own words and pictures.

WHO IS THIS RIDICULOUS SUPERHERO ?

Cut out a picture of someone you don't know from a magazine. Paste it here. Invent a ridiculous superhero identity for that person.

SUPERHERO NAME:

SUPERPOWERS:

WEAKNESS:

ENEMY'S NAME:

CATCHPHRASE:

MAKE **THIS** PAGE SCARY.

A BATTLE

Add smells to stink up these cheesy socks and perfume these flowers.

OF SMELLS

Which smell is stronger?

WHAT ARE THEY?

Add your own secret surprises to these pages: stains, smears, gunge, fluff, candy, toys, cake, anything! Challenge a friend to guess what they are or where you found them.

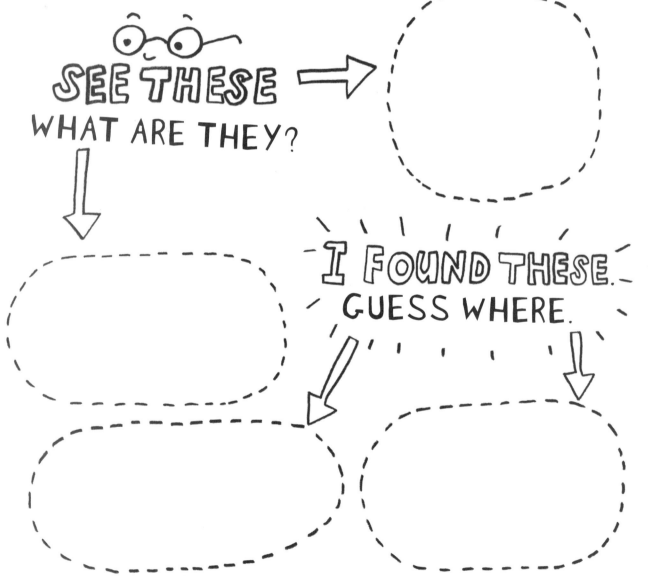

SEE THESE

WHAT ARE THEY?

I FOUND THESE.
GUESS WHERE.

Can your friend guess these, too, but by touch and smell? Get them to try it blindfolded.

FEEL THESE.
WHAT ARE THEY?

SMELL THESE.
WHAT ARE THEY?

THIS IS FOR JOURNEYS

This is like eye spy, but better. Which of the things below can you spot, hear, or feel on your journey? Circle them as you go. On your next journey, circle them in a different color.

GENUINE SNEEZE

STRIPY SOCKS

OLD MAN

LAUGHTER

WORDS IN DIRT

SOMEONE DANCING

SOMETHING STICKY

SQUEAKING SOUND

RED SQUARE

CLOUD THE SHAPE OF A FISH

YELLOW TRUCK

HORSE

GREEN CIRCLE

TOMATO

BOREDOM

GLASS BUILDING

CRYING CHILD

CLOTHES ON A LINE

SMELL OF BURGERS

AN IDIOT

MASSIVE TREE

WHITE SHOES

BLUE LIQUID

ANGRY PARENT

DOG'S TONGUE

WINGS

PURPLE CAR

A BEEPING SOUND

DIRTY BAG

WALKING FLY

BILLBOARD FOR A MOVIE

RIDERLESS BIKE

BLUE SPOTS

ARCHED WINDOW

SKATEBOARD

BLACK CAT

ORANGE T-SHIRT

BAD SMELL

THIS PAGE IS FOR . . . **BUBBLE WRITING**

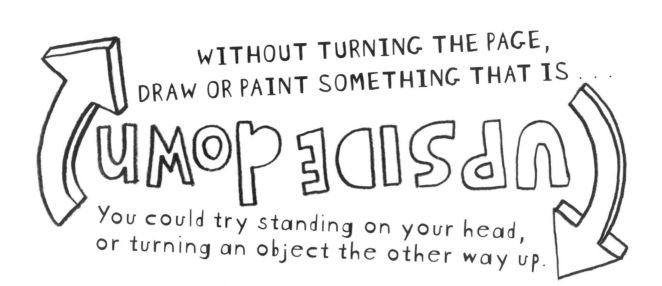

WITHOUT TURNING THE PAGE,
DRAW OR PAINT SOMETHING THAT IS . . .

(UPSIDE down)

You could try standing on your head, or turning an object the other way up.

LEAVE A SURPRISING MESSAGE ON THIS PAGE.

STICK IT SOMEWHERE UNEXPECTED FOR SOMEONE TO FIND.

MAKE A TRAIL OF ARROWS TO YOUR MESSAGE.

WATCH QUIETLY TO SEE IF ANYONE FOLLOWS THEM.

ADOPT

THIS ➡️  BOOK

AS YOUR PET

Staple some cotton balls, pocket lint, or hair to this book, and stick some eyes on it. Attach a leash to it. Give it a name and adopt it as your pet.

Take it for walks.
Teach it tricks. Feed it.

Record the number of weird looks you get from passersby here:

DRIP ON THIS

Drip paint onto these pages. Make a picture in "plops" and in "splats."

Take a small, unimportant
object: an eraser, a pen cap,
a paper clip, etc. Examine it
closely – use a magnifying
glass if you wish. Draw a bit
of it to fill this whole page.
Make it important.

PATTERN THESE
UNDERPANTS.

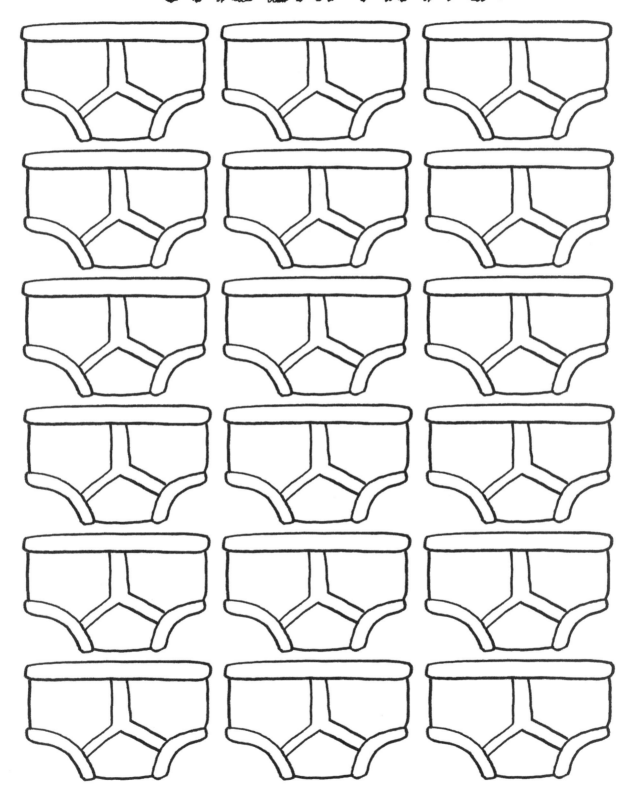

MAKE EVERY PAIR DIFFERENT.

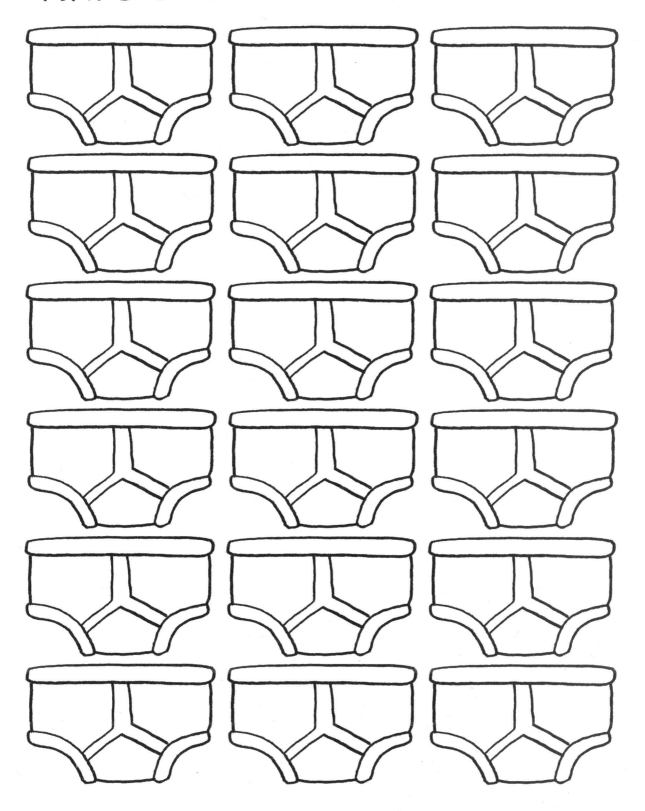

Take the book outside. Drop or toss a pen or marker, and try to land it on these pages to make a mark. Can you draw from far away? Make a pattern from your marks, add scoring areas if you wish, or challenge a friend to a draw-off. Make sure there's no one in the way when you throw.

FEEL THIS

This is a page to be enjoyed by your fingers, not by your eyes. Gather textures, including fabrics, and glue them on. Cover the page with them.

Look UP and draw what you see.

STAND SOMEWHERE YOU'VE NEVER STOOD BEFORE . . .

Look DOWN and draw what you see.

DRIVE THIS

Close your eyes and race around this track with a pen, pencil, or paintbrush. Time yourself – there's a five-second penalty if you go off track. Switch tools or colors and race again to improve your lap times, or challenge a friend. Create racing art.

Make These Up

Here are some made-up words and their meanings.
Add some more of your own.

WORD	MEANING
JAMSTEWING	Wearing your socks for weeks at a time.
HANDROID	Someone who is always putting their hand up in class.
CRIGGLING	Giggling and crying at the same time, such as when being tickled.
BEDCRUSTER	Someone who avoids taking a bath, and goes to bed muddy.
CRUMGE	What you find left at the bottom of the cup after a dunked cookie falls into your milk.
E-LATIONSHIP	Knowing someone only via e-mail or on a social network.
SNUDGE	The mark left on a window after you've pressed your nose up against it.
Farfle	when you mess up
Foobeo	when a fart scares someone

WHAT'S PUZZLING YOU?

What could be tricky to put back together?
Draw something confusing. Cut it out.

ROLL ON THIS

ROLL A COIN TO SCORE!

30 POINTS

20 POINTS

50 POINTS

40 POINTS

10 POINTS

COLOR IT!

Try flipping the coin! Try tiddlywinks!

BRUSH THIS

Swap your paintbrush for another kind of brush: an old toothbrush, nailbrush, hairbrush, or even a broom. Use it to make a picture with movement in it by brushing on paint in different directions.

SHAPE-SHIFTERS

Using only the shapes below,
what can you design?

15 seconds... GO!

Draw each thing below as many times as you can in fifteen seconds. Challenge a friend to try — who can draw the most? Color this page afterward.

The letter X   The letter S   The number 8

Lightning bolts   Circles   Spirals

String   Worms

TIME'S UP!

Sheep   Eyes

question this?

Make up your own ridiculous questions to these answers:

QUESTIONS

ANSWERS

. . . . One second.

. . . . It's massive!

. . . . My friend . . . .
THEIR NAME

. . . . Incredibly annoying.

. . . . NEVER!

. . . . $7,613,756.

. . . . Gross.

. . . . ME!

. . . . Old and stinky.

INFECT THIS

What would this page look like
if it had a disease?

TWIST THIS

Can you say these tongue twisters fast, over and over?

"FRESHLY FRIED FISH"   "BACKPACK-STRAP SHOP"

"STUPID SUPERSTITION!"   "A PROPER COPPER COFFEEPOT"

"A CHEAP SHIP TRIP"   "FLASH MESSAGE!"

"FREDDY THRUSH FLIES THROUGH THICK FOG."

"MUCH MASHED MUSHROOM"   "IRISH WRISTWATCH"

"CECILY THOUGHT SICILY LESS THISTLY THAN THESSALY."

"SEVENTEEN SLIMY SLUGS IN SATIN SUNBONNETS SAT SINGING SHORT SAD SONGS."

"WILLIE'S WOODEN WHISTLE WOULDN'T WHISTLE."

"MANY AN ANEMONE SEES AN ENEMY ANEMONE."

"WHICH WITCH WINDS WHITE WEASEL WOOL WELL?"

"JUST THINK, THAT SPHINX HAS A SPHINCTER THAT STINKS!"

"GOOD GARGOYLE BLOOD, BAD GARGOYLE BLOOD."

"FAT FROGS FLYING PAST FAST"   "GREEK GRAPES"

"INCHWORMS ITCHING"   "UNIQUE NEW YORK"

"THREE FREE THROWS"

ANIMATE THIS

Hold the book and flick
JUST THIS PAGE back and forth.
Remember to add your own sound effects!

HOLD PAGE HERE

Run paint down this page in different colors.
Let it dry. Add more.

PUNISHMENT:

COUNT THESE

HOW MANY?

- Black squares ......
- Triangles ......
- White squares ......
- Black hearts ......
- White things ......
- Semicircles ......
- All things ......

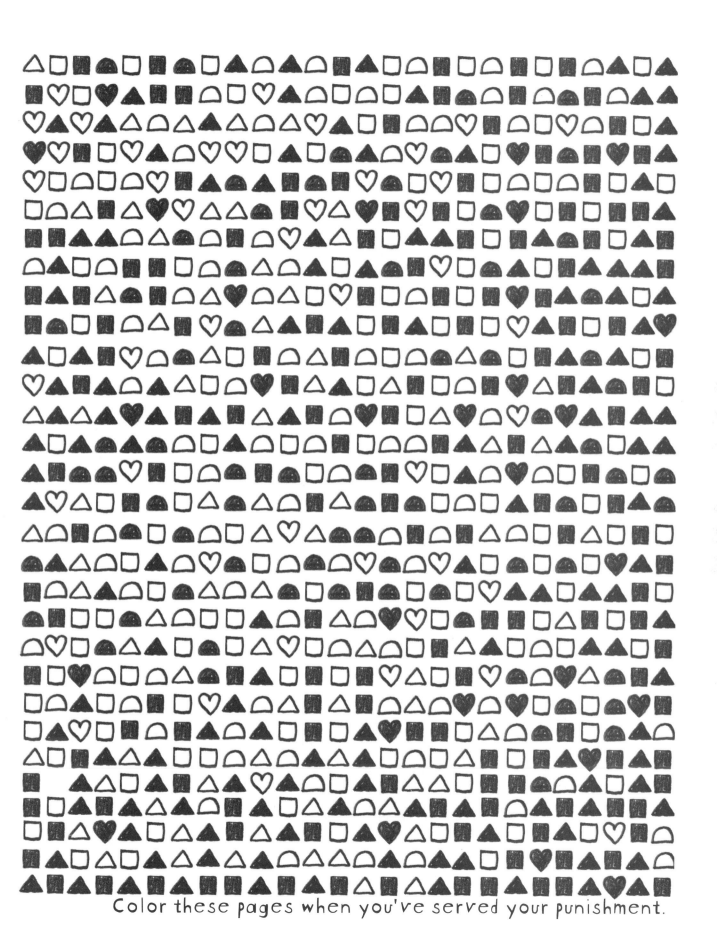

Color these pages when you've served your punishment.

DON'T EVER TURN BACK TO THE PAGE BEFORE

How would this page look if it was a tissue
and you had blown your nose on it?

LOST

Make a poster for something imaginary or silly that you've lost, e.g., a pet insect, a ghost, a smell, or your voice. Offer a reward asking people to find it.

TATTOO THIS

Draw how your tattoo would look if you had one.

Where would it be?

PATCHWORK

Make a patchwork quilt on these pages. Glue on squares from plastic bags, packaging, junk mail, rags, and fabric — but not from your mom's best dress!

ASK this

ATTACH THIS BOOK TO A CLIPBOARD TO MAKE YOU LOOK IMPORTANT. SEE IF ANYONE CAN ANSWER THESE QUESTIONS AND ANY MORE YOU HAVE.

1. What's the opposite of opposite?

2. How long is a piece of string?

3. Who DID let the dogs out?

4. How fast is fast food?

5. Why did the chicken cross the road?

6. What disease did cured ham have?

7. Do people yawn in their sleep?

8. What was the best thing BEFORE sliced bread?

9. If you try to fail, and succeed, which have you done?

10. Can I borrow your car?

DRAW A PICTURE
WITHOUT TAKING YOUR
PEN OFF THE PAGE.

BETWEEN THESE PAGES

TO SANDWICH IT FOREVER.

MOUTHS I FOUND

TALKING

Tear out mouths from magazines.
Glue them here. Add speech bubbles.
What are they saying?
Are they cracking jokes?

EYES I FOUND LOOKING

Tear out eyes from magazines. Glue them here.
Add something unusual for them to look at.

Glue cereal onto this page.
Add images from the cereal box, and even drops
of milk if you wish — this is breakfast art.

CHOOSE YOUR NAME

Rename yourself.
Choose one from each column:

FIRST NAME	MIDDLE NAME	LAST NAME
Captain	Sparrow	Skullhead
DJ	Cool J	Ironfist
Emperor	Awesome	Blurgh!
Awesome	Mac	Chickenplucker
JZBC	Jelly-legs	The First
One-eyed	Pepper	The Invincible
No-pants	Bigfoot	Splatit
Cool	Vlad	Hornetsnest
Agent	Willy	McPants
Wild	Humungous	Wacko
Luscious	G-Ride	TV
Professor	Bling	of Everything
Big	Pants	Sidebottom
Major	Awesome	Von Winkle
King	Burger	Power
Nefertiti	Wobbling	Star
Princess	Hairy	Headrot
Officer	Brains	Umbrella
Xerxes	Thor	The Second
Lord	Wizz	Pox
MC	The Man	Thunderthighs
Doctor	Wriggler	Wallywilly

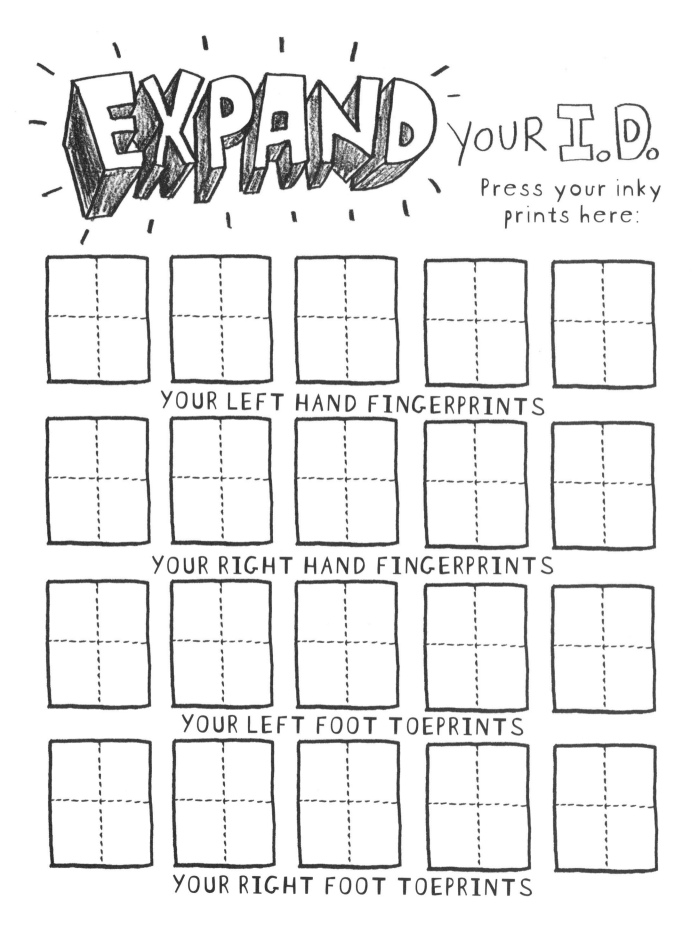

EXPAND YOUR **I.D.**
Press your inky prints here:

YOUR LEFT HAND FINGERPRINTS

YOUR RIGHT HAND FINGERPRINTS

YOUR LEFT FOOT TOEPRINTS

YOUR RIGHT FOOT TOEPRINTS

Pick one of your fingerprints or toeprints
and blow it up to enlarge the pattern in it.
Use the grid to help. Add color if you want.

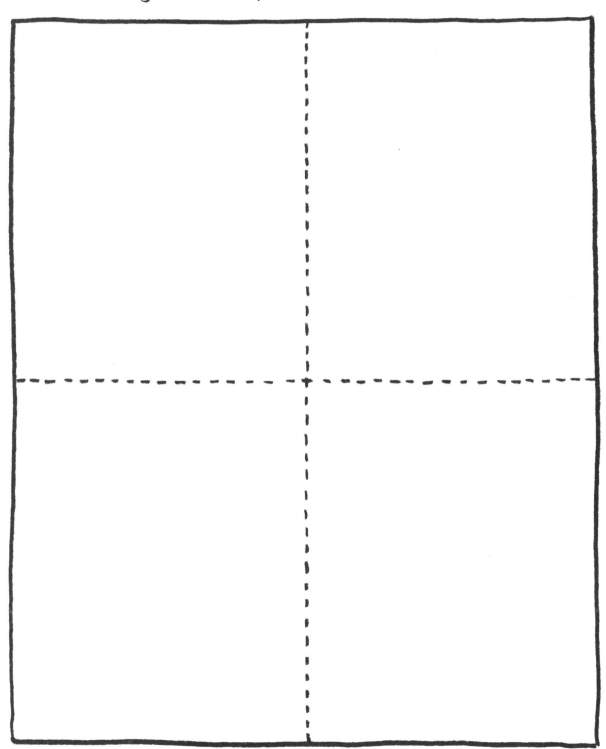

BOX THIS

Divide this page into boxes. Divide some of those boxes into more boxes. Fill boxes. Stack boxes.

WHO TURNED OUT THE LIGHTS?

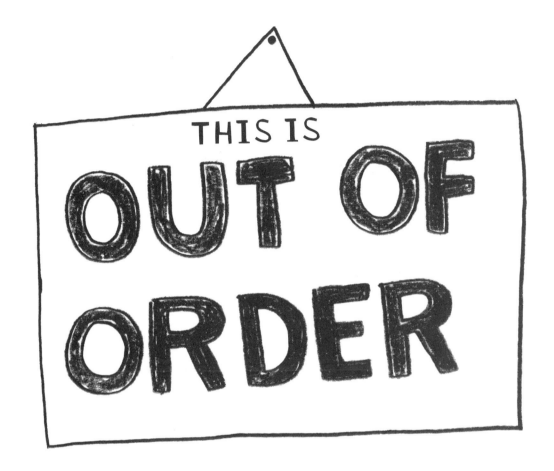

Make it out of order.

MEND THIS

How would this page look if it had been attacked by sharks then stitched back together in the hospital?

ALPHABET COLLECT

Collect a bit of something beginning with each letter and glue it here. If you can't find it, draw it.

A	B	C	D	E
F	G	H	I	J
K	L	M	N	O
P	Q	R	S	T
U	V	W	X	Y
				Z

NUM3ER TH15

Think of a number between 1 and 10.
Multiply it by 2. Take away 5. Add 20. Take away 6.
Multiply it by 1.45782939. Divide it by 0. Give up.
Create a picture by filling this page with numbers.

SECRETLY TAPE A NOTE SOMEWHERE.

SNAIL TRAILS

How would this page look if snails slid across it?
Add your own slime trails, or leave it outside with
lettuce on it to attract some for real.

PUSH YOUR BIKE

MAKE MARKS WITH ITS WET AND MUDDY TIRES.

ACROSS HERE

BEST DONE OUTDOORS IN THE YARD.

HAND THESE OUT . . .

The person now holding this is a
....

likes **YOU**

THIS ENTITLES YOU TO NOTHING. PLEASE COLLECT IT AT 3:30pm

PLEASE LOOK AFTER THIS.

I COUGHED ON **THIS**.

THE ANSWER IS
....

YOU'VE WON A FREE GIFT!
How to claim your gift:
Go to the end of the road, wave your arms, shout "I want my free gift!" cry, do a robot dance – are you still reading? Then write to the President and say please could he send you a puppy. Your free gift is inside it. Wait for it to do one.

YOU like
....

Write or draw some of your own.

SPIN AND GET DIZZY

NOW TRY TO DRAW STRAIGHT LINES.

Do this where there is lots of space
and you won't bump into anything.

HA HA BONK

Draw lines pairing each joke with its correct punch line. Color the shapes you make. Find the rogue punch line – there's one extra!

In their sleevies.

No idea.

What did one string say to the other?

Who was in the bathroom with Tigger?

What do you call a hippie's wife?

Why do birds fly south in the winter?

I'm a frayed knot!

What do you call cheese that's not yours?

Where you left it.

Why is six scared of seven?

Burple.

Invisible bananas!

Pooh.

Because pepper makes them sneeze!

A carrot.

What kind of ears do trains have?

Between you and me, it smells.

Why did the squirrel cross the road?

E-clipse it!

What color is a burp?

Mississippi.

Because seven eight nine.

A ewe turn.

Why do fish live in salt water?

Why did the boy stare at the orange juice?

Where do you find a one-legged dog?

What's orange and sounds like a parrot?

To a retail store.

How do you kill a circus?

What do you call a deer with no eyes?

Engineers.

Nacho cheese.

What was the sheep doing in the car?

What did one eye say to the other?

To show his girlfriend he had guts.

Go straight for the juggler.

Because it's too far to walk!

Because it said concentrate.

Where does a cat go if it hurts its tail?

Where do generals keep their armies?

How does the moon cut his hair?

FOOD ART

Rather than wipe your jelly knife on a napkin, wipe it on these pages. Perhaps add the last scrapings of peanut butter from the jar. Paint and collage with food scraps that are normally thrown away: fruit and vegetable peel, eggshells, burned toast, left-over gravy. It's food art. It won't last forever — it may go moldy and shrivel up. Take photos to record it changing before you have to throw it away.

emotions

Journal your emotions as you feel them. Pile them up.

Make some more of your own.

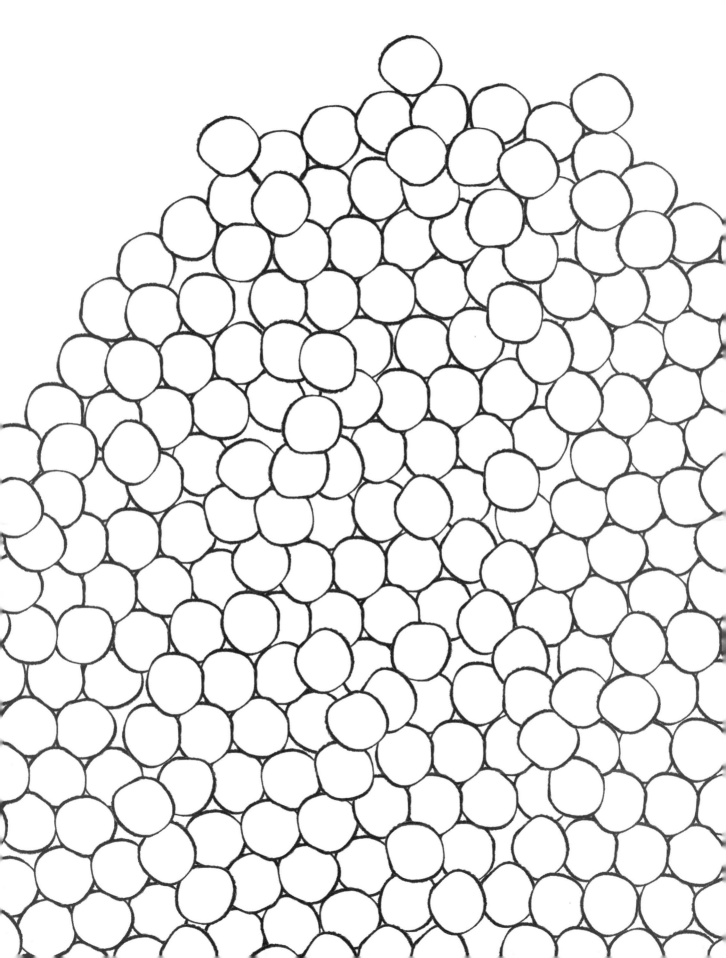

THESE PAGES ARE

A BATTLEFIELD . . .

Color this page.
Tear into tiny pieces. Celebrate!

THIS TICKLES

Make this page as tickly as you can.
Add feathers or poke through wiggling fingers.
Tickle someone with it.

JOIN IN: CREATE ASTEROIDS!

SWAP THIS

Sign this page with your name to identify it. Then swap it with your friend for the same page of their book, and tape theirs here — they will need a copy of this book, too!

. . . .

Add your head.

Add your friend's head.

Fill this with TRIANGLES

Any way you like.

THINGS YOU LIKE

Stack things you like here: in words and pictures.
Decorate them joyfully.

THINGS YOU DON'T LIKE

Stack things you don't like here: in words and pictures.
Splatter them with colors you hate.

SMEAR **THICK WET** PAINT

ON THIS PAGE, **THEN CLOSE**

THE BOOK TO MAKE A  PRINT

When your print is dry, give it eyes, arms, and legs.

GO DOTTY

Create a picture from just dots - lots of dots!

WOULD YOU RATHER...

- ○ Sneeze at the end of every sentence?
- ○ Squeak when you speak?

- ○ Be armor-plated?
- ○ Be fireproof?

- ○ Have ears made of cheese?
- ○ Always stink like onions?

- ○ Your parents still dress you as a baby?
- ○ Your teacher is now dating your mom?

- ○ Never eat a burger again?
- ○ Never eat ice cream again?

- ○ Be able to fly?
- ○ Be able to read minds?

- ○ Have a lifelong nosebleed?
- ○ Have lifelong hiccups?

- ○ Eat someone else's booger?
- ○ Eat someone else's earwax?

- ○ Have donkey ears?
- ○ Have fish eyes?

- ○ Come in at the top of the class?
- ○ Hold the world record for juggling?

- ○ Be the richest person in the world?
- ○ Be the best-looking person in the world?

- ○ Fight a bear?
- ○ Fight a lion?

- ○ Have a beard full of maggots?
- ○ Have hair crawling with spiders?

WANTED

NAME . . . .

CRIME . . . .

REWARD . . . .

Make a WANTED poster for a criminal.
It could be someone you know or someone imaginary.
Was their crime against you? Was it something silly?
What's the reward for catching them?

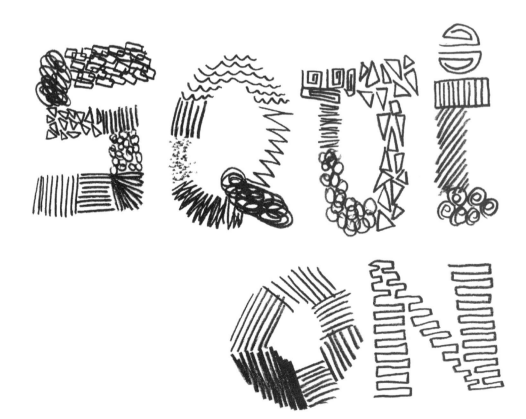

GOOGLE THIS

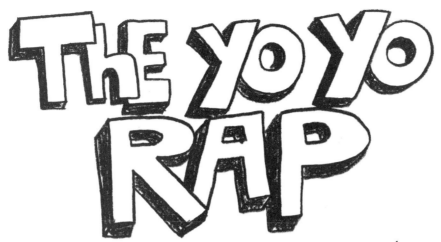

THE YO YO RAP

Finish writing the "Yo yo" rap — the most repetitive and annoying rap in the world. Rap it when the "La-la" song gets banned.

Yo, yo, yo, yo, yo . . .

WRAP
THIS

Make this page like wrapping paper.

MUMMIFY THIS

Mummify this page – add bandages.
Use toilet paper or draw them on. Are eyes
peering out, or is gunk leaking from between them?

GROAN!

THESE PAGES ARE YOUR DOORMAT.

Ask people to wipe their shoes on them on the way in. NO DOG DOO!

Whose footprints are whose?
Get everyone to sign their own.

COME

COME ON IN. MAKE YOURSELF AT HOME.

GATHER SEEDS, GRAINS, AND POLLEN HERE:

Wet the page here.
Add mustard seeds.
The seeds will grow if
you keep the page damp.

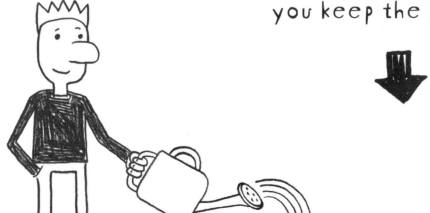

SPARE FINGERNAILS

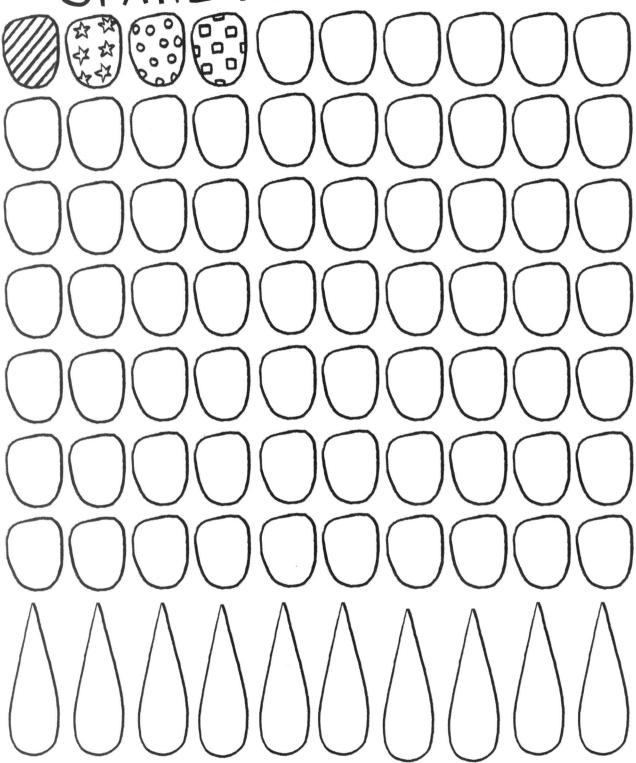

Bling them, paint them, or make them dirty and rotten.

THIS PAGE IS YOURS TO
DECORATE

WRITE THE **TRUTH** HERE — WHAT YOU REALLY **THINK** ABOUT SOMETHING:

NOW BURY **IT!**

CREATE A MAP SHOWING WHERE THE TRUTH
IS BURIED — X MARKS THE SPOT.

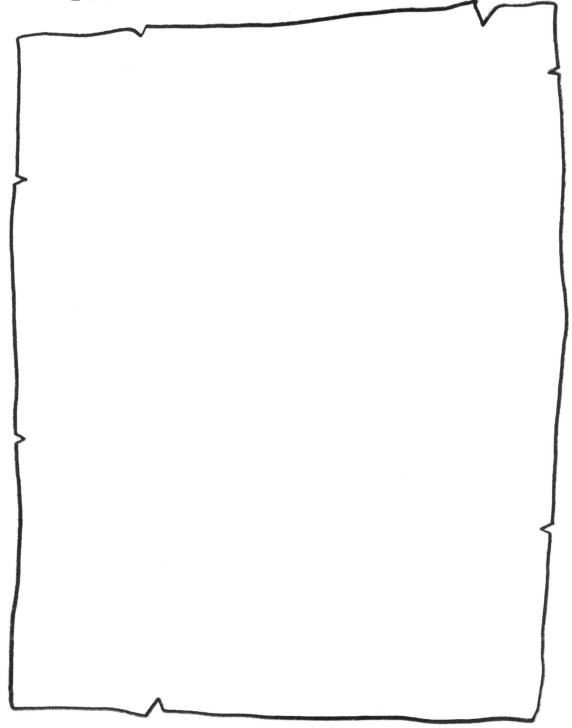

Stain your map with coffee or tea to make it look old.

BLOW THIS

Blow a picture onto these pages.
Use paint and a straw or bubble blower, or hang the
book up in the wind with glue on it and see what sticks!

MAKE A
FAN

Color this page as you like.
Fold it one way, then the
other, over and over, to
make a fan, like this:

Use this page to be a fan of something you think is GREAT! Celebrate it here! It can be anything you like: a sports team, a celebrity, your mom or dad, a place, or even yourself. Go crazy for it in words, drawings, and cutouts.

Look carefully at these pages. Close the book, then try to recall what's here. How many things can you remember? Add others of your own, then try again a few more times. See how your memory improves!

THIS IS THE PAGE

Find the word **THE** in magazines and newspapers and collect it here, over and over.

The word **THE** works well because you'll find it lots, but if you'd rather use other words, like DORK or DOG or DENDROCHRONOLOGY, go right ahead!

DENDROCHRONOLOGY is the study of the rings of a tree.

WATER BOMB!

Start with a square of paper.

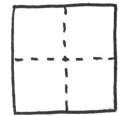

1. Fold it in half horizontally, then unfold. Fold in half vertically, then unfold.

2. Turn it over. Fold it diagonally in both directions, then unfold.

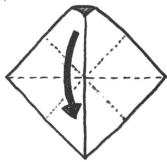

3. Fold the top corner to the bottom. Do not unfold.

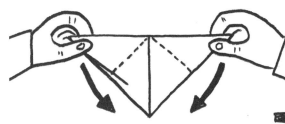

4. Pinch the corners and push them together to look like step 5.

5. Press it flat.

6. Fold the upper layer's corners A and B to point C.

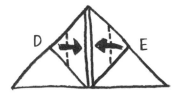

7. Fold the upper layer's side corners D and E to the center.

8. Tuck the loose top points into the small triangular pockets created in step 7.

9. Turn it over. Repeat steps 6, 7 and 8 for the reverse. It will then look like this.

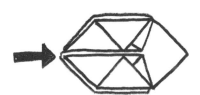

10. Locate the end opening and blow hard into it to inflate.

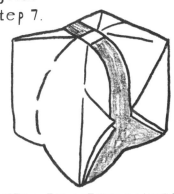

FILL IT WITH WATER!

Lay a cloth behind this page.

Add spills and color. Let them blot. Decorate with stains and dirty finger marks.

Whatever

you write or draw here

will come **TRUE**.

CRYSTAL BALL

KEEP A CRAZY DIARY OF DUMBNESS FOR ONE WEEK.

Note the crazy or dumb things you do, see, hear, or say during one week — include falling over, forgetfulness, and fashion disasters.

THURSDAY

FRIDAY

SATURDAY

SUNDAY

TAKE THIS BOOK TO SCHOOL AND GET ALL YOUR
FRIENDS TO SIGN THESE PAGES OR WRITE YOU
A SHORT MESSAGE - keep these forever to
remember everyone when you are old.

APPLY A FACE MASK

Face masks might include chocolate, mud, or avocado.

USE THIS BOOK AS A BAT

How FAR can you bat a ball?
. . . a scrunched-up piece of paper?
. . . a leaf?
. . . a rotten tomato?
How HIGH can you bat a ball?
. . . a feather?
. . . a boiled egg?

How many times can you bounce an apple?

Take the book outdoors.
Challenge a friend to
book baseball or
book table tennis.

TOK

Cover this page in spirals: long, short, painted, drawn, stuck on, or cut out.

CRAZY

What's the longest spiral you can tear? Hang it up.

REPORT THIS

This is your report card. What would your teachers say about you?

Best teacher is . . . .

Teacher you'd most like to slime is . . . .

HAVE YOU EVER . . .

- ◯ Fallen asleep in class?
- ◯ Forgotten your gym clothes?
- ◯ Pretended to be sick to try to get a day off?
- ◯ Copied?
- ◯ Been praised?
- ◯ Had an "accident" in class?
- ◯ Been sent out?
- ◯ Had to hide in the bathroom?

ARE YOU GOOD AT?

- ◯ Spelling
- ◯ Making friends
- ◯ Science
- ◯ Being on time
- ◯ Acting
- ◯ Sports
- ◯ Art
- ◯ Making people laugh
- ◯ Bragging
- ◯ Math
- ◯ Not getting caught
- ◯ Music
- ◯ Looking good

What's your best excuse for not doing your homework?

What do you think you'll be when you're 30 years old?

THE WORLD'S WORST PHOTOS

Add the worst photos you can find . . .

START YOUR OWN COUNTRY.

FIRST, DESIGN YOUR FLAG.

Tape it to a pole.

Write down YOUR rules for YOUR country:

- -

- -

- -

- -

- -

Write down the name of anyone who breaks your rules and who is banned from your country:

Collage candy wrappers here.
It's a good excuse to eat candy!

ROLL THIS INTO A PEASHOOTER

PHHT

Shoot scrunched-up bits of paper.

MAKE THIS A

HAIRY PAGE.

Add yarn, hair, string, cotton, etc.

Keep adding to this page from one day to the next. Go over things or erase them. It will change as you change your mind. It will never be finished.

KEEP DOING THIS

DRAW it LIKE it is

In this book some words are drawn descriptively, such as **HEADACHE**, **RUNNY**, and **STRIPY**. Try drawing words of your own, or have a go at these: SPLAT, SHATTER, BANG, PRETTY, WOBBLY, SPOTTY, MESSY.

STACK UP STICK MEN

DRAW HOW YOU'D LOOK AS A FLOWER

↓

BUILD IT

Design a building that you'd like to live in.

CRUMB COLLECTION

Use tape to collect crumbs here.

NOSE PAINTING

Paint using only your nose. Hold your hands behind your back and get up close: Splotch with the tip and smear with the sides.

AND THE Winner IS...

Color these ribbons, then award them to your favorite page, your second-favorite page, and your thirteenth-favorite page.

LISTEN TO THIS...

Oooh, baby, baby!

Write the lyrics to a song you like. Illustrate them by drawing images the song makes you think of, then decorate them in a style that suits the mood.

MAKE THIS BOOK . . .

TALK

Turn any page into a ventriloquist's dummy for a comedy act.

1. Fold a piece of paper in half.

2. Fold it in half again.

3. It should look like this.

4. Fold it lengthwise to crease it, then unfold.

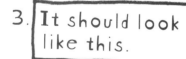

5. Fold the ends to the center.

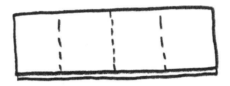

6. It should look like this:

7. Stand it up, with the center creased, and slide your fingers into the openings at the top and bottom.

8. Draw on eyes or weird features. Decorate as you wish.

DO THIS WITHOUT MOVING YOUR LIPS:

It's easier to say some words than others. With your mouth a bit open but not moving, say the vowel sounds: A, E, I, O, U. These are easy.

Now try these letter sounds: B, F, V, P, M, W. These are impossible. Ventriloquists switch them: B to D, F to TH, V to TH, P to T, M to N, W to OO.

So "bogey" becomes "dogey,"
"funny" becomes "thunny,"
"very" becomes "thery,"
"pick" becomes "tick,"
"money" becomes "noney,"
"water" becomes "ooater."

The audience doesn't notice because it's focused on the dummy's moving mouth.

Practice in front of a mirror. Move your dummy's mouth with each syllable.

HEY, WHO YOU CALLING A DUMMY?

MASH-UP

Combine each pair of pictures to make something funny.

Draw here:

girl's face

custard pie

boy in underpants

ants

running man

banana peel

FEED THIS

Tear a hole here for this mouth. See what weird things you can fit through it: food, paint, objects, words, crayons, pens, magazines, stationery, ideas – anything you want. Write down on this page everything you feed it.

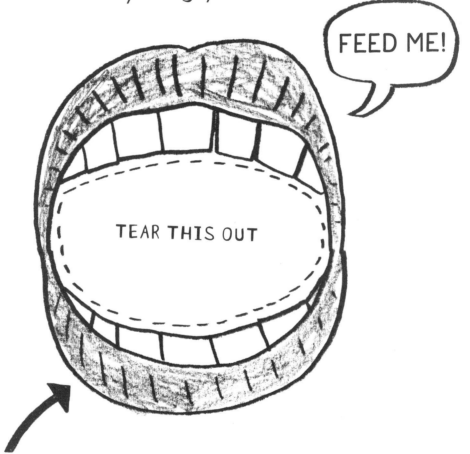

FEED ME!

TEAR THIS OUT

Draw something dribbling from the lips.

DO YOU WANT FRIES WITH THAT?

Everything you fed this book is now being churned up here, in a stomach. How would everything look being mixed together?

NOTE THIS

Cover this page in sticky notes, draw a picture, then rearrange the notes.

TAPE THIS

Create a picture here using tape. Pattern the tape or use different colors and widths. Tape objects on or tape over them to make bumps and ridges.

!!¥∠*/@?!

DESIGN THIS

Design your own T-shirt with a slogan.

LOOKIN' GOOD

BLACK AND WHITE

Fill this page with anything that's black and white.
NO COLOR!

In the two speech bubbles, write down part of a conversation you overhear: people talking in class, at home, or on TV. Now look around and draw two random objects you can see, one below each bubble.

THIS IS SILENT

Use this page to communicate your needs for the next hour without speaking.

Scatter things on these pages: cake crumbs, the letters of your name, or anything you feel like. Draw ripples around each thing until they meet and fill the pages.

DRAW AROUND YOUR LEFT HAND WITH YOUR RIGHT HAND.

PUT SOMETHING SQUISHY
NOW CLAP THE

DRAW AROUND YOUR RIGHT HAND WITH YOUR LEFT HAND.

IN EACH HAND YOU'VE DRAWN.
BOOK **TO SPREAD IT**.

THE SPECTRUM

BLINDLY TEAR OLD MAGAZINE PAGES INTO TINY BITS.

Now sort the bits by color. Paste them here in a spectrum pattern to fill both pages: reds progressing to oranges to yellows to greens to blues to purples.

SPONGE THIS

Use a sponge to paint.
Smear it, dab it, throw it.

ONE DAY, WHEN YOU BECOME
FAMOUS, THIS BOOK OF YOUR
DRAWINGS AND THOUGHTS
WILL BE WORTH MILLIONS.

Try to sell this page cheaply now to someone,
explaining that it's a good investment.
Draw something they might like: Ask them their
favorite colors and use those, or draw a picture
of them. Sign it and swap it for cash — even just one
penny proves you can turn your ideas into money.

One minute...GO!

You have just one minute to draw each
thing below as many times as you can:

Star

Stick man

Tree

Spider

Mouse

Cat

Beast

Vehicle

Building

QUIT
DAWDLING,
DORK!

0:59

Trap

Invention

THINK OF A ROOM THAT
YOU'RE NOT IN NOW.
TRY TO DRAW **IT** FROM MEMORY.

Go and check how you did.

Now redecorate and fill the room to make it **MUCH MORE EXCITING**.

TO REMEMBER A RAINY DAY.

Color a picture of anything you can see out of the window. Take it outside in the rain so the colors run. Leave it to dry.

NOTICE This...

Make a notice that's so bright and bold EVERYONE will notice it. It could be an announcement, a slogan, a message, an ad, or just a word.

Save this page for a special moment:
for when you are feeling inspired, or when
you are incredibly bored. Or for when you
really want to do something in this book again.

MEASURE THIS

HOW TALL IS THIS BOOK? . . . .

HOW TALL ARE YOU? . . . .

HOW HEAVY IS THIS BOOK? . . . .

HOW HEAVY ARE YOU? . . . .

HOW MANY PEOPLE HAVE HELD IT? . . . .

HOW MANY PEOPLE'S NAMES ARE IN IT? . . . .

HOW MUCH DID IT COST? . . . .

HOW MUCH DO YOU EARN? . . . .

HOW FAR HAS IT TRAVELED? . . . .

HOW MANY PAGES ARE IN IT? . . . .

HOW MANY PAGES HAVE YOU DONE? . . . .

HOW LONG HAVE YOU HAD IT? . . . .

HOW FAR CAN YOU THROW IT? . . . .

HOW MANY OF YOUR THOUGHTS ARE IN IT? . . . . .

HOW MANY OF YOUR FRIENDS HAVE SEEN IT? . . .

HOW COOL IS IT? . . . .

HOW COOL ARE YOU? . . . .

HOW OFTEN ARE YOU IN TROUBLE? . . . .

HOW UNFAIR IS THAT? . . . .

While you're thinking, color in all the "O"s above.

COLOR THESE!

MAKE THEM ALL DIFFERENT.

SAUCE ART

Make a ketchup painting — or use chocolate
sauce or mustard, if you prefer.

IT POOED ON THIS!

An enormous hungry beast has eaten everything in the art shop: pens, paints, paper, crayons – everything!

What would this page look like if it pooed on it?

OH, MAN!

IMAGINARY
PERSONAL TRIUMPHS

HOORAY!

Describe or draw what happened on these great days:

The day you won a gold medal.

The day you were on TV.

The day . . . .

Describe or draw what happened on these terrible days:

IMAGINARY PERSONAL DISASTERS

OOPS!

The day you threw up in class.

The day you forgot your clothes.

The day . . . .

SHARE THIS

Get as many people as you can to draw on these pages, all at once, until they're full.

ARGUE FIERCELY

Select two different art tools, such as a pen and a paintbrush. Make them argue with each other in marks and scribbles. Draw the noise and the shouting.

GRRR!

HOLD THIS

Make a holder for pens, art materials, or even liquid.
It won't last long with liquid in it — and don't drink
from it if you've painted it beforehand.

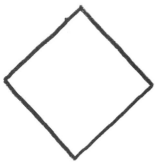

1. Decorate a square, about 6 inches across. Place it decorated side down.

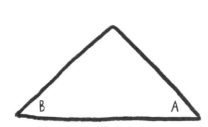

2. Fold it into a triangle with the decorated side visible.

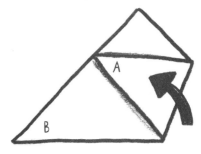

3. Fold corner "A" to its opposite edge, meeting it at about 90°.

4. Fold the top corner of the front layer downward.

5. Turn it all over and, on the reverse, fold corner "B" upward to its opposite edge.

6. Also on the reverse, fold down the top corner of the remaining layer.

7. Use your fingers to open up the holder. Fill it.

CLASH THIS

Draw or cut out things that clash and combine them in a picture — things that DON'T belong together.

Tear junk mail into large pieces.

Paste them over this page, layer upon layer.

Now tear strips away to look like

layers of old ads on a billboard.

SHOOTING GALLERY

Take the book outdoors and paint these pages
using a squirt gun and water-based paint.
If you want, involve a friend for a "shoot off."

THE SAD PAGE

This page is for your sad thoughts.
Decorate them to cheer them up.
Use it as a tissue for tears.

BOO-HOO

POINT WITH THIS

Point the way, point something out, or make your point with this:

PICK AN EVENT THAT HAPPENED TO YOU. TURN IT INTO A NEWS STORY WITH A HEADLINE AND A PICTURE.

Name of newspaper:

Headline:

What happened:

Photo:

DESIGN THREE BOOKMARKS.
Mark where you are in the book,
the most revolting page, and the silliest page.

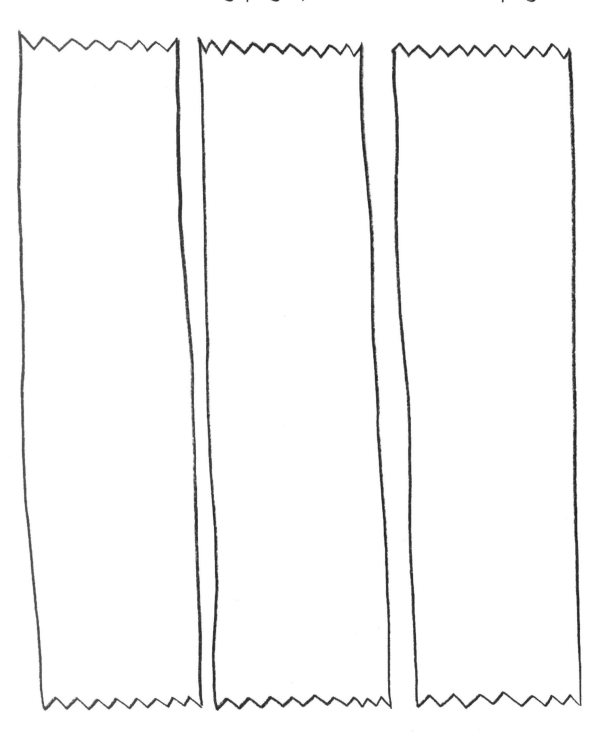

Make a new cover for this book and glue
it onto the back. Call it anything you want.
Be the author if you like.

RE-COVER THIS BOOK

Turn the book back to front
and upside down to switch
between the two covers.
Convince people
you are reading
something different.

ONLY FOR GENIUSES bY ME

EXAMINE

THESE

Can you spot the difference between these pictures? (Answer on the last page.)

Things to release onto these pages might include:
a pet cat with dirty paws, a dog, the dog's fleas,
your burps, your frustration, your imagination.

A BOW **TIE** A DAY FOR A WEEK

Refine them.
Design your own
the way you like
to wear them.

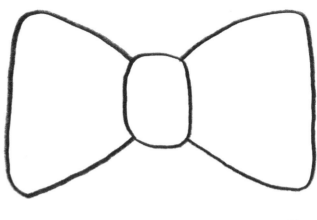

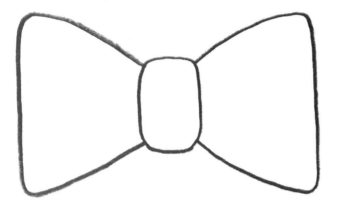

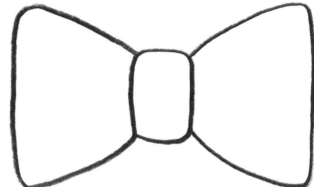

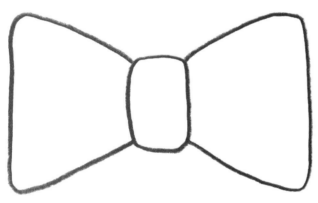

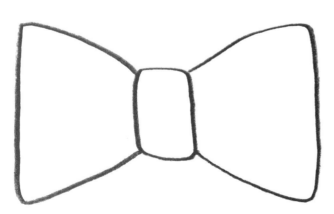

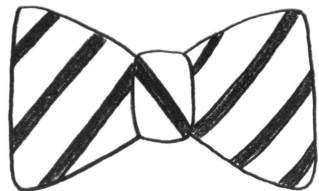

MAKE-UP THIS

Add tribal paint or make-up.

OR ZOMBIE MAKE-UP!

Make these pages gross.
What looks gross to you?

PERFORM THIS

Magic torn paper back together again!

Back of sheet 2

Start with two identical sheets of plain paper (sheet 1 and sheet 2).

Scrunch sheet 1 into a ball. Hold it behind the top corner of sheet 2 with your left hand. Show sheet 2 to the audience and say, "I will rip up this sheet of paper then magic it back together."

With your right hand, tear sheet 2 to pieces. Pass each loose piece to your left hand, keeping them in front of the screwed-up ball of sheet 1.

Now scrunch the loose
pieces forward to
create a second ball
in front of the ball
you've been hiding.

Holding the two balls
together, turn them around
as you blow on them and say
a magic word: "Abracadidiot!"

Hold up both balls again,
now with ball 1 at the front.
Slowly unfold it, keeping the
ripped ball 2 hidden behind it.
Hey presto — the paper
appears intact again!

THIS CREASES
ME UP!

Back of
sheet 1
unfolding

MELT IT

Choose any object that you like the look of.
Draw it as if it is melting.

HELP, I'M MELTING!

What I think about me:	What other people think about me:

ROCK THIS

Start a band. Think of a name for it.
Make a poster advertising your first big concert.

If people turn up and you don't
know how to play any instruments,
just act cool and say the
band has had to split because
of "artistic differences."

RECORD THE SOUNDS YOU CAN MAKE WITH THIS PAGE OR BOOK.

CRUMPLE

RUSTLE

RRRIIIIIIPP!

WHACK!

you are a stinky cucumber

What are the most ridiculous phrases you can make using these words?

lice boyfriend amazing break bad answer
my pie six pick whatever runs wash bald
scab burps cats fish sausage that boring has
what squishy of awesome green house boy
chocolate are rat bottom face a burst you
lemons hairy squashes elephant banana fluff
wet monster electric dad haunted never with
pants like moldy fire prince their bears
happy exploded are ate bendy her did scary
spot not are liquidized toffee of so my you
a rules robber your like going my toilet on
I alone trouble afraid all and fairies there
is in big up I your gross like jelly made poo
a pulsating berserk went large are the brain
being fantastic pig suck an my day dream a
I and naked our the of he by hit it girl a
a leg gorilla sore mom am has a a are the
a pants dog on is is

Rearrange the words into
ridiculous phrases here:

BARCODE ART

Gather bar codes from packaging. Combine them here in a design.

CLONE THIS

Draw in multiple colors by holding colored
pencils or felt-tipped pens in a bunch.

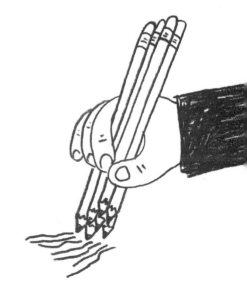

INJURE THIS

How might this page look if it were injured? Perhaps something would be oozing from it, or would it have a huge scab on it? It may look broken, bruised, stung, or scarred. It may need a cast. You choose.

THIS ISN'T A NUMBER 8.

8

It's part of something else. **YOU** decide what it is.

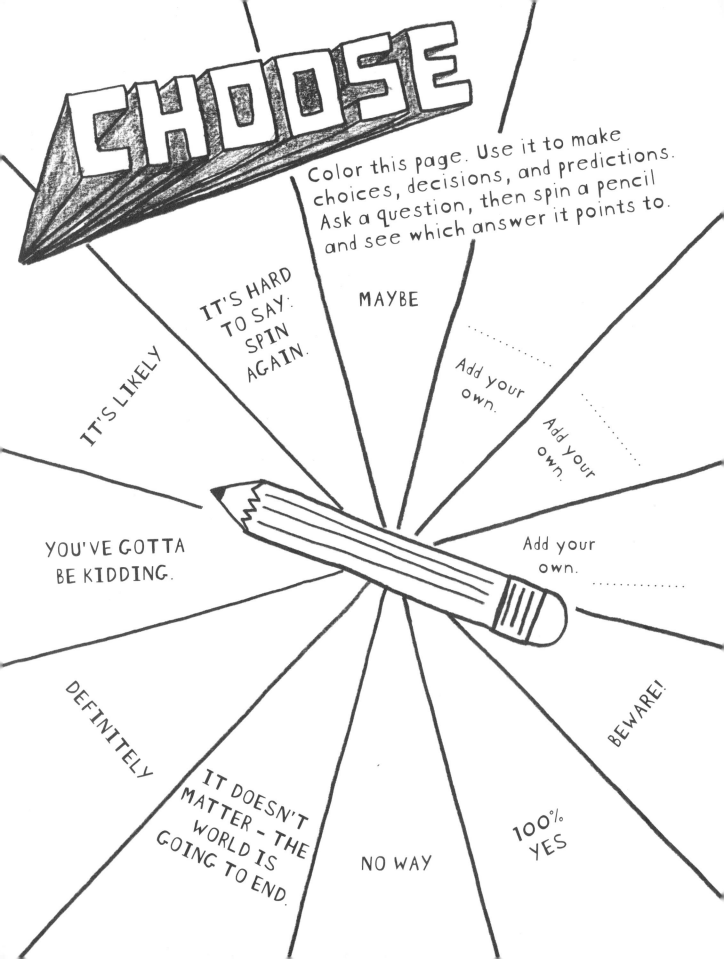

THIS IS A STICK-UP!

Color these. Stick or tape them where you like.

THIS IS A **SIGN** OF THINGS TO COME →

IF YOU'RE READING THIS, THEN YOU'RE A . . . .

HANDS OFF

LOOK BEHIND YOU

Temporary SIGN

LOSER

SPLAT

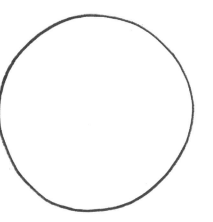

Cover this page in pencil. Use an eraser
to draw or write a ghostly message.

Mini MASTERPIECES

Search through this book for mini masterpieces hidden within your pictures. Find small sections to cut out and hang here in your gallery, or draw new ones. Hold a mini exhibition.

BACK TO Front

Stick notes onto your face with words on them that describe you. Now draw yourself in the mirror.

THIS IS MAGIC

Fairies go here.
Slam the book shut to squish them.

IN ANY WAY YOU WANT . . .